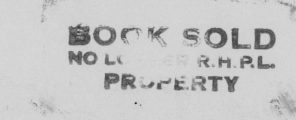

Health
and
Wellness

Eve Hartman and Wendy Meshbesher

Raintree

Chicago, Illinois

www.heinemannraintree.com
Visit our website to find out
more information about
Heinemann-Raintree books.

To order:
☎ Phone 888-454-2279
💻 Visit www.heinemannraintree.com
to browse our catalog and order online.

©2009 Raintree
an imprint of Capstone Global Library, LLC
Chicago, Illinois

Edited by Adam Miller, Andrew Farrow, and
 Adrian Vigliano
Designed by Philippa Jenkins and Ken Vail
Original illustrations © Capstone Global Library
 Limited 2009
Picture research by Ruth Blair
Originated by Raintree
Printed in and bound in China by South China Printing
 Company Ltd.

13 12 11 10 09
10 9 8 7 6 5 4 3 2 1

Library of Congress Cataloging-in-Publication Data
Hartman, Eve.
 Health and wellness / Eve Hartman and Wendy
Meshbesher.
    p. cm. -- (Sci-hi. Life science)
 Includes bibliographical references and index.
 ISBN 978-1-4109-3326-3 (hc) -- ISBN 978-1-4109-
3334-8 (pb) 1. Health. 2. Self-care, Health. 3. Hygiene.
I. Meshbesher, Wendy. II. Title.
 RA776.H29 2009
 613--dc22
                    2009003462

Acknowledgments
The author and publishers are grateful to the
following for permission to reproduce copyright
material: © iStockphoto/Günay Mutlu contents pp.
iii (contents top); © iStockphoto/Jose Manuel Gelpi
Diaz pp. **iii** (contents bottom); © iStockphoto p. **5**; ©
Blend Images/Alamy p. **4**; © EDELMANN / SCIENCE
PHOTO LIBRARY p. **6**; © iStockphoto/Leigh Schindler p.
7; © iStockphoto/Maciej Bogacz p. **8**; © iStockphoto/
Jose Manuel Gelpi Diaz p. **9**; © iStockphoto/Michael
DeLeon p. **9**; © Compassionate Eye Foundation/Sam
Diephuis/ Getty p. **10**; © iStockphoto/daniel rodriguez
p. **11**; © iStockphoto/Catherine Yeulet p. **13**; ©
STEPHANIE SCHULLER / SCIENCE PHOTO LIBRARY p.
15 (top); © CONEYL JAY / SCIENCE PHOTO LIBRARY
p. **15** (bottom); © BIOLOGY MEDIA / SCIENCE PHOTO
LIBRARY p. **17**; © iStockphoto/cecilie johanse p. **16**
(left); © Science Photo Library p. **16** (right); © WILL &
DENI MCINTYRE/SCIENCE PHOTO LIBRARY p. **18**; ©
SAMUEL ASHFIELD/SCIENCE PHOTO LIBRARY p. **19**;
© SHEILA TERRY/SCIENCE PHOTO LIBRARY p. **21**; ©
Andrew Twort/Alamy p. **23**; © David J. Green - Lifestyle
/ Alamy p. **24**; © UpperCut Images / Alamy p. **27**; ©
iStockphoto/Graça Victoria p. **29**; © iStockphoto/
Aleksey Puris p. **28**; © iStockphoto/Thomas Shortell
p. **30**; © iStockphoto/Günay Mutlu p. **31**; © HEALTH
PROTECTION AGENCY / SCIENCE PHOTO LIBRARY p.
32; © superclic / Alamy p. **34**; © JIM VARNEY / SCIENCE
PHOTO LIBRARY p. **35**; © PR. M. BRAUNER / SCIENCE
PHOTO LIBRARY p. **37**; © Science Photo Library p. **37**; ©
JUPITERIMAGES/ Thinkstock / Alamy p. **39**; © Bubbles
Photolibrary / Alamy p. **41**; © Shutterstock background
images and design features.

Cover photograph of a teenage girl reproduced
with permission of © Punchstock/Photographers
Choice **main**; cover photograph of medicine tablets
reproduced with permission of © Alamy/B.A.E. Inc.
inset.

The publishers would like to thank literacy consultant
Nancy Harris and content consultant Ann Fullick for
their assistance in the preparation of this book.

Contents

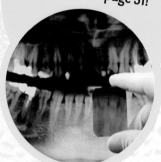

Why do dentists take X-rays of your teeth? Find out on page 31!

How tall would this infant be as an adult if she kept growing at the same speed that she's growing now?

Turn to page 9 to find out!

Some words are shown in bold, **like this**. These words are explained in the glossary. You will find important information and definitions underlined, <u>like this</u>.

HEALTH AND WELLNESS

What is the most complicated and powerful object that you use every day? The answer is your body. The human body is made of more parts than a typical machine, and it does more tasks than any computer.

Yet like a machine, the human body needs to be used and cared for properly. **Taking care of your body is one of the keys to a long, healthy life.** This book will present many facts about the human body and the best ways to care for it.

What is the human body?

The human body is an example of an **organism**, or individual living thing. Like other organisms, the body is made of tiny units called **cells**. It has perhaps ten trillion cells. Ten trillion is a 1 with 13 zeros after it! That's 10,000,000,000,000.

The body's cells are highly organized. Similar cells join together to form **tissues**. A variety of tissues make up a body part called an **organ**. The heart and liver are examples of organs. Organs across the body may work together as **organ systems**.

We know more about the way our bodies work now than ever before. But new discoveries are still being made!

4

TASKS FOR ORGAN SYSTEMS

Every organ system performs a specific task. The circulatory system, for example, includes the heart, blood vessels, and blood. Blood vessels carry blood through the body as it circulates (moves through the body on a closed path). The circulatory system brings food and oxygen to all body cells, and it removes wastes. The nervous system includes the brain, spinal cord, and nerves. In the nervous system, the spinal cord and nerves carry messages to and from the brain. The brain then controls other organ systems.

The body's organ systems work together to maintain all body functions. In a healthy body, every organ system works at its best.

When exercising, the circulatory system kicks into high gear. The system rushes extra blood (which contains oxygen and nutrients) to the parts of the body that are working the hardest. The circulatory system even helps regulate body temperature!

The Early Years

Although every human life is unique in many ways, all humans share many of the same experiences. <u>Humans pass through characteristic stages of growth and development.</u> Before birth are the stages of pregnancy, during which the body develops from a single **cell**. Infancy and childhood are the first stages after birth.

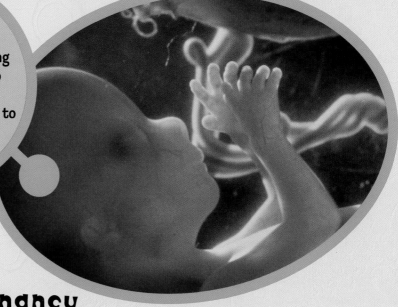

A healthful diet, exercise, and avoiding alcohol and tobacco all help a pregnant woman to give birth to a healthy baby.

Early pregnancy

A woman who is carrying a developing baby is described as pregnant. A pregnancy typically lasts about 9 months.

The first cell of a new human forms when a male reproductive cell, or sperm cell, joins a female reproductive cell, or egg cell. The new cell quickly begins dividing. It forms 2 cells, then 4 cells, then 8 cells, and so on.

The growing mass of cells is called an **embryo**. After about a week, the embryo attaches to the wall of the **uterus**. The uterus is a chamber in the female reproductive system.

From fetus to baby

The body's shape begins to appear during the embryo stage. Early forms of the spine and brain also begin to form. **At about 8 weeks, the embryo becomes a fetus. This is when organs and organ systems develop.** Many organs begin working.

When a baby is born, the lungs breathe air for the first time. Quickly the baby uses the mouth and digestive tract, typically by taking milk from the mother.

A HEALTHY PREGNANCY

During a pregnancy, the developing baby depends completely on the mother. If the mother practices healthful habits, it is likely that the baby will be healthy, too.

A pregnant woman should avoid alcohol, tobacco products, and certain drugs and medicines. Each can pass from the mother's blood supply to the baby's blood, where it can cause much damage.

Infancy

Compared to many baby animals, a newborn human is especially weak and helpless. A newborn can move arms and legs, but cannot crawl or walk. The newborn also needs liquid food, which ideally is milk from the mother.

The infancy stage lasts from birth until about age 1. **An infant changes greatly during the first year, more so than during any year that follows.** The infant grows about 25 centimeters (10 inches) and triples in weight. Bones harden and muscles develop. The brain learns how to use these muscles to move the body. The infant also learns to recognize new words and faces.

As an infant changes into an older baby, both the infant and caregivers face many challenges. Gradually the baby learns to communicate with words, eat solid food, and use the toilet.

Childhood

Very young children are called toddlers because of their unsteady walk. The hips and legs have not yet fully developed.

The bodies of children grow and develop every year. Children also learn new knowledge and skills, and they forge friendships and family relationships. Although children learn to take care of themselves in many ways, they still depend on their parents or guardians.

With each passing year, an infant or child learns new skills and develops more independence. The first year brings the greatest changes to the body.

BABY TEETH

Most organs grow gradually during childhood to take on their adult sizes. Teeth are a big exception. Baby teeth develop early and help with chewing and speaking. They also hold space in the jaw for permanent teeth. Beginning at about age 6, permanent teeth push out the baby teeth above or below them. Permanent teeth are meant to stay in place for life!

SPEED GROWTH

Human bodies develop at an incredible rate during their first year. If a typical infant kept growing at the first year growth rate, that person would reach adulthood with a height of about 5 meters (16 feet)!

Adolescence and Adulthood

As children approach their teen years, their bodies begin to change in new ways. This stage of life is called **adolescence**. <u>During adolescence, the body develops new male or female traits.</u> These **traits** include further development of the reproductive system.

Puberty and adolescence

The time that adolescence begins is called **puberty**. Most girls reach puberty between ages 9 and 13. Most boys reach it two years after the girls do. In both genders, however, puberty may be entered a little before or after the typical range.

<u>Puberty occurs because of changes in the levels of estrogen or testosterone.</u> **Hormones** are substances that cause **cells** to grow and develop in certain ways. Estrogen is the hormone in girls. It comes from the ovaries, which are the female reproductive organs that produce eggs. Testosterone is the hormone in boys. It comes from the testes, which are the male reproductive glands that produce sperm. Both hormones **stimulate** reproductive organs to develop. Estrogen also triggers the onset of the **menstrual cycle**, or period. This is the monthly cycle of the female reproductive system.

At age 10, many girls have entered puberty while boys have not. The girl in this picture has begun to grow toward her adult height. The boy will probably have to wait a few years to begin his growth spurt.

More changes

Estrogen and testosterone also stimulate secondary sexual characteristics. These are traits apart from the reproductive organs but still specific to gender. Female traits include breasts and wide hips. Male traits include facial hair and a deep voice.

Other changes of adolescence include the growth of body hair under the arms and in the pelvic region. The body also grows significantly taller, an event called a **growth spurt**. By the end of adolescence, the body has reached its adult height.

By age 18, boys and girls have nearly completed adolescence. Their bodies have acquired male or female adult traits. By this time, boys have had their chance to go through a growth spurt, too.

Changing minds

Adolescence also brings changes to the mind. Many adolescents feel self-conscious or embarrassed about the changes to their bodies. Mood swings are common during this stage, as are a variety of feelings about the opposite gender.

Adolescents often are tempted by risky actions and behaviors. Yet many begin to look at their lives in more mature and abstract ways. They may make serious plans for their lives as adults.

Adults

Adulthood is the mature stage of human life, meaning that all body systems are fully developed. For much of adulthood, the body may change very little from year to year.

As the adult body ages, however, body systems gradually slow down and use less energy. Adults who continue eating habits from their teenage years are prone to weight gain, especially if they do not exercise sufficiently. In many sports, athletes typically pass their peak abilities in their twenties or thirties.

As an adult woman ages, she will eventually reach menopause, which is the time when the menstrual cycle stops. Menopause often occurs between ages 45 and 55. After menopause, a woman is not able to become pregnant.

Senior adults

By the 60th year, the body has slowed greatly and has changed in many ways. Hair has turned gray, eyesight has become poorer, and wrinkles line the face. The body is also more prone to injury and disease.

Nevertheless, the minds of senior adults can be as sharp as ever. With a healthy mind, people can lead active lives at any age.

SENIOR ATHLETES

As well as having sharp minds, many senior adults continue to enjoy athletic lifestyles well past their sixties. New improvements in medical science help make it possible for people to stay healthy and active further into their lives. Every year senior athletes in the US can enter to compete in the National Senior Olympics. There are 25 events—everything from swimming to basketball to triathlon! The Senior Olympics began in 1987 and has now grown to have over 10,000 competitors. In 2007 the oldest athletes at the games were over 100 years old!

LIFE EXPECTANCY

One hundred years ago, people often died before age 50. Today, the average person in the United States lives to about age 78. improved sanitation and health care are the major reasons why people now lead longer lives.

The oldest known human life lasted 122 years. Scientists have evidence that the body cannot last for much longer than this. <u>Eventually, body cells lose the ability to reproduce. Without new cells to replace the old, body systems weaken and fail.</u>

Body systems slow as adults age, but senior adults can lead active, healthy lives for many years.

A disease is a condition which affects the ability of the body to function properly. **A wide variety of diseases can affect the body, and the body has many defenses against them.** These defenses are the reason why people stay healthy most of the time, and why they recover after many diseases strike.

Blame the germs!

For most of human history, people had vague or incorrect ideas about the causes of diseases. This began to change when microscopes were invented. By the 1800s, scientists had established that germs cause many diseases. **Germs are microscopic living things or particles that can invade the body.**

Bacteria, fungi, and protists are examples of germs that are alive. Viruses are germs made of genetic material. Genetic material stores the information of a life form and is passed from parents to their offspring. Viruses trick body cells into reproducing virus particles.

SURROUNDED BY GERMS

No matter how hard we try, we humans can't get rid of germs. They swarm over most of the objects we touch everyday. Door handles, keyboards, the bottoms of purses and shoes, and toilet seats have some of the highest numbers of germs. But you'll never guess the germiest of all: cell phones!

Communicable diseases

Germs cause **communicable diseases**, meaning diseases that can be caught. Some communicable diseases are mild, such as colds and athlete's foot. Others are more serious. AIDS is caused by a virus, as is a liver disease called hepatitis.

Germs can spread through air, water, and food. Many spread through close contact with an infected person or animal.

Stopping the spread

Washing with soapy water helps kill many types of germs and stops them from spreading. Covering your mouth when you cough or sneeze also stops the spread of germs.

Keeping kitchen surfaces and equipment clean helps stop food-borne germs. Many foods need to be kept cool or frozen to keep germs from growing on them.

Bacteria live almost everywhere! These colonies of bacteria grew from an ordinary human handprint. The light-colored areas on the hand show the largest colonies of bacteria.

Three lines of defense

The body has three lines of defense to fight invading germs. **When one line of defense fails against germs, the next line is called into action.** These defenses keep you healthy and help you recover from disease.

1

First line

The body's barriers to its environment are the first line of defense. These barriers include skin, tears, mucus in the nose and throat, and acid in the stomach. Most germs cannot pass these barriers alive.

2

Second line

Parts of the blood act as the second line of defense. If germs invade through a cut or scrape, for example, types of white blood cells will try to destroy them. A raise in body temperature, called a fever, helps slow the growth of germs.

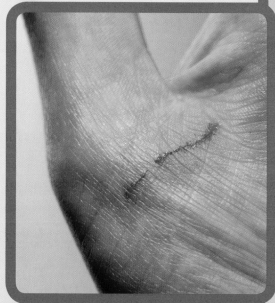

VACCINES

Diseases such as polio and small pox were once common and deadly. Today, the use of vaccines has all but eliminated them.

<u>Vaccines work by preparing the immune system to fight a specific kind of germ.</u> Most vaccines are made from weakened or killed forms of a germ. When the immune system meets the vaccine, it makes antibodies against it. Then, should the real germ invade, the immune system is ready to fight it.

3

Third line

Special types of white blood cells make up the third line of defense, which is also called the **immune system**. The immune system makes **antibodies** in the blood. The antibodies recognize specific germs, and the immune system then attacks and destroys the germs.

When a new kind of germ invades the body, the immune system needs time to make an antibody against it. But then it "remembers" that antibody. A type of germ may cause an illness once, but not if it tries to invade a second time.

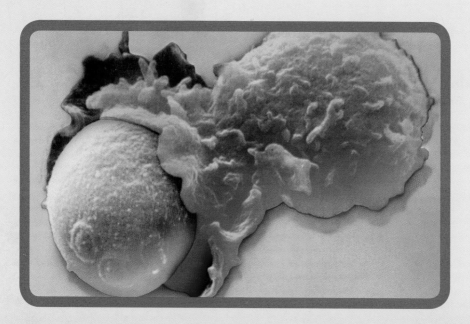

Noncommunicable diseases

Noncommunicable diseases do not spread from person to person, nor do germs cause them. These diseases have a variety of causes.

Some noncommunicable diseases strike when body parts wear out. Arthritis, for example, is caused by worn-out joints, making movement painful.

A poor diet can lead to many diseases. The body needs many vitamins and minerals, and lack of any of them can lead to serious illness. Overeating can lead to disease, too.

Genes carry information for development and are passed down from parents. Diseases may also be inherited through genes. Examples are sickle-cell disease, in which small blood vessels are blocked by crescent-shaped red blood cells. Red-green color blindness, and hemophilia, in which the blood clots poorly or not at all, are also inherited diseases.

Cancer

Cancer is a general term for a variety of noncommunicable diseases that strike across the body. **In a cancer, abnormally-shaped cells grow and divide rapidly.** Typically these cells form a mass or lump called a **tumor**. If left untreated, cancer cells can spread to many body parts.

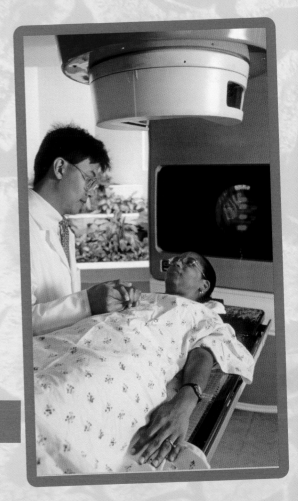

Cancer often strikes randomly. Yet certain behaviors make cancer more likely. Smoking tobacco products can lead to lung cancer. High-intensity sunlight can lead to skin cancer.

Many forms of cancer once were deadly. Now more cancers than ever before can be detected early and treated, and even cured.

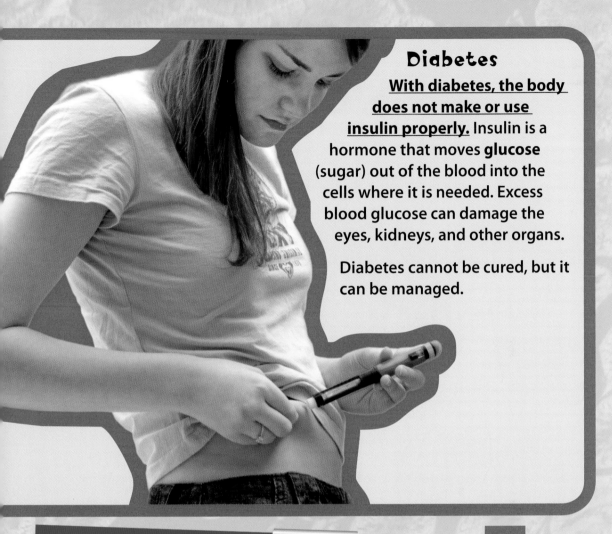

Diabetes

With diabetes, the body does not make or use insulin properly. Insulin is a hormone that moves **glucose** (sugar) out of the blood into the cells where it is needed. Excess blood glucose can damage the eyes, kidneys, and other organs.

Diabetes cannot be cured, but it can be managed.

Disease report

- What diseases are affecting people today?
- What parts of the world are most at risk from West Nile virus and malaria?
- How can we solve deadly problems like antibiotic resistance and hospital infection?

Search newspapers, magazines, and the Internet to find answers to these and other questions that interest you.

Diabetes patients need to monitor their glucose levels carefully. This girl needs to take shots of insulin. This helps to regulate glucose levels in her blood.

Diet and Nutrition

Nutrients are materials in food that the body needs and uses. Your body needs a variety of nutrients, and no single food contains all of them. <u>A wide variety of foods can supply the body with all the nutrients it needs.</u> With the right combination of foods, the body can work at its best.

Many nutrients

Your digestive system breaks down food into tiny pieces. Although the foods you eat may have many tastes and textures, they mostly contain only a few types of nutrients.

Carbohydrates

Sugars and starches are types of carbohydrates. Each carbohydrate is broken down into **glucose**, the **molecule** that the body uses for energy. A molecule is a tiny group of atoms. **Calories** are the units used to measure the energy in food. Most calories in the diet come from carbohydrates.

Proteins

The digestive system breaks down proteins, which are **organic compounds**, (compounds that come from living things) into the **amino acids** they are made of. Amino acids are molecules that are critical to life and play a role in metabolism (body processes that work to use food and nutrients). Cells reassemble the amino acids into new proteins that they can use. Cells need proteins for growth and repair.

Lipids

Oils and fats are made of molecules called lipids. The body needs only certain lipids and in limited amounts, as they are very high in calories. Vegetable oils are a more healthful source of lipids than are animal fats. Lipids are needed in order for the body to absorb certain vitamins.

Vitamins and minerals

The body needs both vitamins and minerals in relatively small amounts. Vitamins help the body perform certain **chemical reactions**, such as regulating cell growth. Minerals help make up healthy cells and body fluids.

Water

The body is mostly water, and it is essential to replace the water your body loses. You can get the water you need either from drinking fluids or from eating watery foods.

Vitamins, minerals, and other nutrients are put into pills or powders. **Nutritionists** sometimes recommend these products to aid, but not replace, a balanced diet.

VITAMINS AND MINERALS

What foods do you eat on a regular basis? Are you getting lots of one kind of vitamin and not much of another? Check out this table to learn more.

Vitamin or mineral	Sources	Purpose
Vitamin A	liver, carrots, broccoli, leafy vegetables	for healthy eyes and skin
B vitamins (such as B_1, B_2, B_3, B_9, B_{12})	potatoes, bananas, many meat and fish products	support the nervous system, immune system, cell growth, and many body functions
Vitamin C	citrus fruits	helps make collagen, a part of skin, gums, and other tissues
Vitamin D	fish, fortified milk, and other products	for healthy bones
Iron	meat, beans, leafy vegetables	for healthy red blood cells
Calcium	milk and dairy products	for healthy bones and teeth

A balanced diet

To help people choose the variety of foods they need, dietitians (experts in diet and nutrition) organize foods into five food groups. **A balanced diet includes foods from each food group.** Together, the food groups provide all of the nutrients the body needs.

Grains group

Grains include wheat, corn, oats, rice, and rye. They are made into breads, pastas, and cereals. These foods supply carbohydrates, the source of energy for the body.

Some experts argue that grains should be kept to a minimum in the diet. According to their reasoning, high levels of body fat and **cholesterol** come from excess carbohydrate in the diet, not excess fat. Cholesterol is a natural compound that is found in most body tissues. But some forms of cholesterol may harden arteries (a condition in which arteries are blocked with fatty deposits).

Meat and beans group

This group also includes fish, nuts, and eggs. These foods are rich in proteins. Many people choose not to eat meat or other animal products. They need to take in proteins from other sources, such as beans and nuts.

Fruits group

Fruits provide many vitamins and minerals not always found in other groups. Oranges, grapefruit, and other citrus fruits, for example, provide Vitamin C. Fruits also provide **dietary fiber**, which is material that helps food move through the digestive tract.

Vegetables group

Like fruits, vegetables also provide vitamins, minerals, and dietary fiber. Leafy vegetables are rich in iron, a mineral needed for healthy blood. Carrots contain a nutrient that the body converts to vitamin A, important for healthy eyesight.

Milk group

This group includes milk, cheese, and yogurt. These foods are rich in calcium, an important mineral for healthy bones and teeth.

Vegetables are very diverse. Each contains nutrients that help a plant survive, and in turn can help people, too.

LACTOSE INTOLERANCE

The sugar in milk is called **lactose**. Many people digest lactose poorly, and are described as lactose intolerant. Many such people can gain the benefits of milk from fermented milk products, which include cheese and yogurt.

Diet challenges

Maintaining a balanced diet depends on three healthful meals a day, including breakfast, lunch, and dinner. Eating is also a social event, and should be enjoyed with friends or family.

For many people, maintaining body weight is one of the biggest challenges for their diet. More Americans today are seriously overweight than ever before. Nutritionists point to many possible causes of this problem, including poor dietary choices, lack of exercise, and the typically poor nutritional content of many processed foods. These foods are sometimes high in fat, salt, or sugar, and low in vitamins and other nutrients.

Teens often are concerned about their body weight. Many try fad diets or other schemes to lose weight. Others eat a very poor diet and suffer from low body weight. These kinds of behaviors are not healthful.

Movies, magazines, and television programs often show "perfect people," whose body shapes are impossible to maintain in good health. Some fashion models have suffered from poor health because of their efforts to remain extremely thin.

Dietitians and nutritionists

If you have questions about your diet or body weight, you can ask a dietitian or nutritionist. These health experts work with people to find the diet that is right for them.

<u>**A dietitian will tell you that body weight cannot be safely gained or lost significantly over just a few days or weeks.**</u> Rather, the key is to combine a healthful, balanced diet with daily exercise and a positive outlook.

Healthy choices?

In the US, fast food accounts for about half of all money made from restaurants. But fast food is gaining lots of popularity in other parts of the world such as Asia and the Middle East. The fast food industry in India is growing by around 40 percent a year!

FOOD LABELS

Labels on food packages list the nutritional value of the food inside them. Compare the labels for five breakfast cereals. Which cereal supplies the most vitamins and minerals? Which supplies sugar and calories you might not need?

Physical Fitness

A body that is **physically fit** is strong, durable, and flexible. **<u>The key to physical fitness is to exercise for at least 30 minutes a day.</u>** Being physically fit also helps people feel better about themselves and sharpens the mind. It even improves sleep!

Aerobic exercise

Scientists classify exercise into two groups. **Aerobic exercise** is performed with moderate intensity over a relatively long period of time. Jogging, biking, swimming, and basketball are examples of aerobic exercise.

The term aerobic means "with oxygen." Aerobic exercise helps muscles use oxygen to generate energy efficiently. It also improves the heart and lungs, as well as muscle tone throughout the body.

Anaerobic exercise

In contrast, **anaerobic exercise** is intense and quick. Weightlifting is one example. Anaerobic exercise helps build up muscle mass and strength.

<u>A healthful exercise plan should include both aerobic and anaerobic exercises.</u> Many trainers encourage people to alternate these two types of exercise from day to day, as well as to alternate the muscle groups being exercised.

Useful exercise can be done alone or in a group, or by playing a team sport. You can choose any form of exercise that you enjoy.

The dangers of anabolic steroids

The term "anabolic" refers to the building up of body tissues. Drugs called **anabolic steroids** can build up muscle mass, acting as an artificial substitute for anaerobic exercise. Yet these drugs have many harmful and dangerous side effects. They include reduced fertility, mood swings, and increased likelihood of injury.

<u>**The use of anabolic steroids and other drugs does not lead to physical fitness.**</u> Any perceived benefit they may bring is far outweighed by their drawbacks.

No one likes to be sick. Even a scratchy throat or a mild rash are annoying. **Keeping the body clean helps prevent many diseases.** The practice of keeping clean is called **hygiene**. Good hygiene helps people look and feel their best.

Preventing acne

Regular washing and bathing are part of good hygiene for people of any age, but are especially important during the teenage years. **Washing the face removes sweat and skin oils, thus helping to prevent a disease called acne.**

Acne is characterized by red or white skin lesions, commonly called zits or pimples. In severe acne, the lesions can become infected and leave small scars.

Preventing body odor

Sweat by itself is odorless. The odor of an unwashed body comes from **bacteria** (single-celled, microscopic **organisms**) that live on the skin and that sweat helps promote. **Washing regularly with soap and water helps stop body odor.** Also helpful are antiperspirants, which are chemicals that reduce sweat. They are used under the arms, where sweat often collects.

Antiperspirants come in different strengths, odors, and styles of application. While useful, they are not a substitute for daily washing.

28

ACNE

Acne is common during adolescence because of the body's rising levels of sex hormones. Some of these hormones trigger glands in the skin to release more sweat and skin oil. They combine with dead skin cells or other tissues to clog a pore.

Some research suggests that a diet rich in fats and sugars can promote acne. if so, it is yet another reason to avoid "junk food," such as soft drinks, candy, and extra-sweet baked goods.

Acne is a common disease of adolescence. Many medications help fight acne. Only in severe cases is a doctor's help required for treatment.

Cavities and gum disease

Food is fuel for the body. Unfortunately, it also is fuel for bacteria. **Many kinds of bacteria live in the mouth and can do much damage there.** The damage begins when bacteria invade the teeth or gums.

A cavity is a bacterial infection of a tooth. Most cavities are confined to the **enamel**, which is the hard outer layer of a tooth. If the infection grows, however, it may spread into the root of the tooth. Such infections can be quite painful.

An infection of the gums is called **gingivitis**. If it is allowed to continue, it may eat away at the gums until teeth literally fall out.

Oral hygiene

The best way to prevent infections to the teeth and gums is to practice good oral hygiene. Oral hygiene includes thoroughly brushing teeth after meals, cleaning teeth and gums with dental floss, and gargling with mouthwash. These practices clean the mouth and slow the growth of bacteria.

Dentists are experts on oral hygiene. Seeing a dentist at least twice a year will help you keep a healthy mouth.

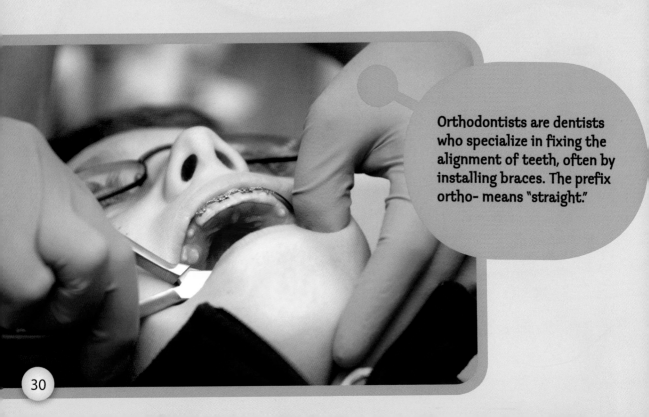

Orthodontists are dentists who specialize in fixing the alignment of teeth, often by installing braces. The prefix ortho- means "straight."

TWO SETS OF TEETH

Everyone gets two sets of teeth. The first set of 20 teeth is called the baby teeth. Beginning at about age 6, these teeth are replaced by a set of 32 teeth, called the adult teeth or permanent teeth.

Permanent teeth sometimes do not enter the mouth correctly. They often are pushed forward or backward, or off slightly to one side. Braces on the teeth can help fix this problem.

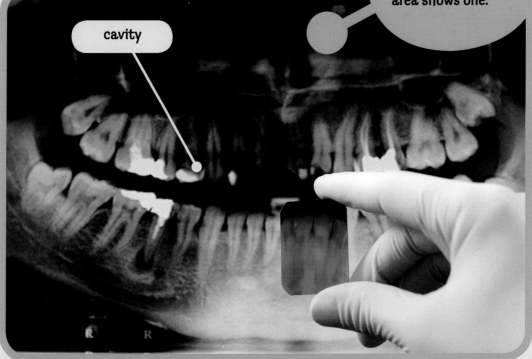

Dentists take X-rays to find hidden cavities. The dark area shows one.

cavity

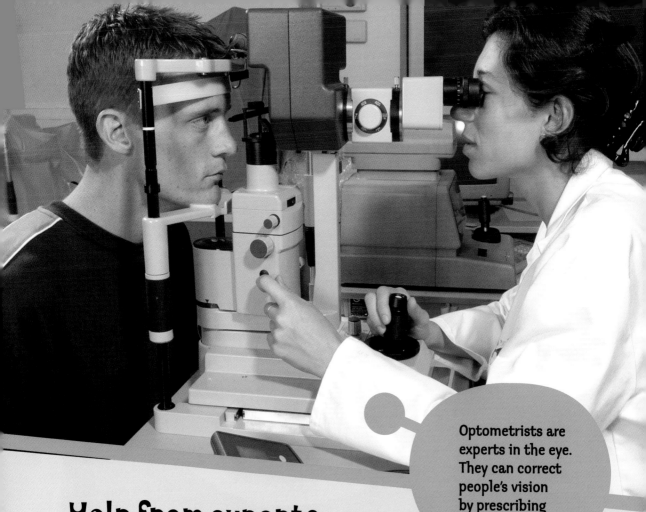

Optometrists are experts in the eye. They can correct people's vision by prescribing eyeglasses.

Help from experts

If you feel sick or hurt, ask for help from a parent, teacher, or other trusted adult. Do not ignore sharp pains or expect them to go away on their own. Pain shows that a body part is injured and needs rest and attention. Ignoring pain could lead to a more serious illness or injury.

When symptoms are serious, you may need attention from a physician or other health care expert. A physician is the leader of a health care team. Other team members include nurses, medical technicians, therapists, and pharmacists.

Nurses are health care professionals who work under the supervision of doctors. Medical technicians are usually trained to perform certain medical tests. Therapists help people recover from injuries and illness. And pharmacists make sure patients get the medicines that doctors recommend.

MEDICAL SPECIALTIES

Most physicians pursue a specialty, meaning they treat only certain types of patients or certain diseases.

Specialist	Treats
Cardiologist	heart disease
Endocrinologist	diseases of glands
Gastroenterologist	the digestive system
Nephrologist	kidney diseases
Ophthalmologist	eyes and vision
Orthopedist	bone diseases and injuries
Pediatrician	children
Surgeons (many types)	many diseases and injuries through surgical operations

Medicines

A **drug** is any substance that changes how the body functions. A **medicine** is a drug that is intended to improve body functions. Some medicines improve only the symptoms of disease. Aspirin relieves pain, for example, but does not fight the disease or injury that causes the pain.

Other medicines treat the disease itself. **Antibiotics**, for example, kill or damage invading bacteria. Penicillin, erythromycin, and cephalosporins are examples of antibiotics. Some other types of medicine are part of **chemotherapy**, a treatment used to kill cancer cells.

Aspirin and other mild medicines are available for any adult to purchase. They are **over-the-counter** medicines, and are sold at drug stores and supermarkets. Stronger medicines, however, are available only from a doctor's order. They are **prescription medicines**, so named because a doctor must prescribe their use.

ALCOHOL, TOBACCO, AND DRUGS

Alcohol, tobacco, and certain illegal **drugs** each change the way the body functions. A user may find their initial effects to be pleasing. Unfortunately, these substances cause much damage, especially with repeated use. They are **addictive**, meaning they can make the user want more of them. The body might even need more of the substance to maintain itself.

<u>Users of alcohol, tobacco, or drugs can easily become addicted—and find their addictions difficult to break.</u> These addictions have ruined many lives.

Alcohol

Alcohol is a chemical that depresses the **nervous system**. Although beer and wine have a lower percentage of alcohol than hard liquor, the alcohol in each is the same substance.

<u>The higher the level of alcohol in the blood, the more the nervous system is affected.</u> Even moderate levels of alcohol will slow reaction time, which is why a person should never operate a motor vehicle after drinking alcohol. High levels of alcohol typically cause drastic changes of mood, slurred speech, and impaired ability to think and reason.

Liquor companies use slick, appealing ads and packaging to sell their products. Your health and welfare is not their main concern.

Alcoholism

Long-term abuse of alcohol can permanently damage the brain, stomach, liver, and other body organs. It also leads to **alcoholism**, a disease that involves both a physical and emotional dependence on alcohol.

Without alcohol, the nervous system of an alcoholic produces shaking, seizures, and hallucinations (false visions). Alcoholics find themselves losing control of their lives, as alcohol becomes more important than their jobs or school, friends, and family.

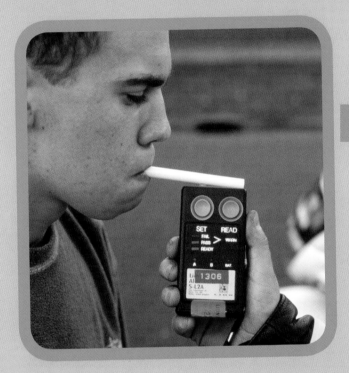

This teen is being tested for alcohol with a breathalyzer device. Any person caught driving after drinking alcohol faces severe penalties, including the loss of driver's license.

Recovering from alcohol abuse

If you or a family member suffers from alcohol abuse, help is available. Many clinics and treatment centers help people break the hold of alcohol on their lives. In addition, an organization called Alateen helps teens cope with family members who abuse alcohol.

Tobacco: it's not "cool"

Many people once thought that smoking was a stylish, clever habit. Yet scientific studies have shown that using tobacco products is risky and dangerous—not "cool" at all.

Tobacco products include cigarettes, cigars, and chewing tobacco. Each contain **nicotine**, a drug that **stimulates** (excites) the nervous system. It is also highly addictive, especially among teens. <u>Teens who begin a tobacco habit often develop a lifelong addiction.</u>

Harm from tobacco

The burning of tobacco produces over 4,000 chemicals, many of which are harmful. Tobacco smoke also creates a thick, sticky substance called tar. Tar builds up in a smoker's lungs, where it often leads to a thick voice and a hacking cough. Smoking causes diseases such as emphysema, which brings shortness of breath as the lungs become less elastic, and lung cancer.

Tobacco use can also damage the heart and **circulatory system**, as it leads to the hardening of arteries. It can damage the mouth, teeth, and bones, and even discolor the skin. Smokers often appear pale and in ill health. They are poor athletes, too.

Tobacco warnings worldwide

SMOKING CAUSES MOUTH AND THROAT CANCER
Australia

SMOKING SEVERELY HARMS YOU AND THE PEOPLE AROUND YOU
Austria and Germany

SMOKING CAUSES HEART DISEASE
Russia

SMOKING CAUSES AGEING OF THE SKIN
Ireland

SMOKING DURING PREGNANCY HARMS YOUR CHILD'S HEALTH
France

WARNING: CIGARETTES CAN CAUSE LUNG CANCER
85% of lung cancers are caused by smoking
80% of lung cancer victims die within three years
Canada

SMOKELESS TOBACCO

Smokeless tobacco includes products called snuff and chewing tobacco. They are designed to be chewed or sucked. The user spits out the dark, tobacco-stained saliva that accumulates.

Unfortunately, smokeless tobacco is just as harmful as cigarettes and cigars. Long-time users may lose their teeth, gums, and even large parts of their face to cancerous tumors.

SECONDHAND SMOKE

You can suffer the bad effects of tobacco just from being near where it is used. **Secondhand smoke** enters the air from a burning cigarette or cigar, or from the mouth of a smoker. This smoke contains a huge number of chemicals, many of which are poisonous or cause cancer. Lawmakers cite the dangers of secondhand smoke for the banning of smoking in restaurants, offices, and other public places.

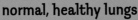
normal, healthy lungs

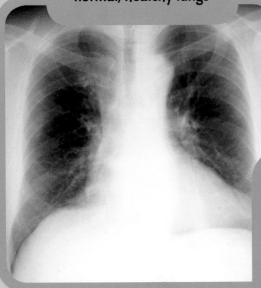

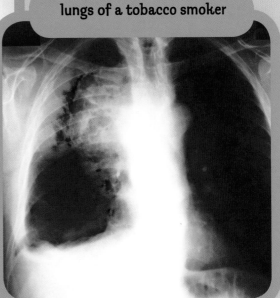
lungs of a tobacco smoker

Tobacco products contain poisons that damage the lungs and other organs.

Drug abuse

Any drug can be abused, meaning used improperly so it harms the body. **For especially dangerous drugs, even a single dose can cause great damage.** Moreover, many drugs are very addictive.

MARIJUANA

Marijuana comes from the cannabis plant. Its active ingredient passes into the brain and affects thought, sensory perception (how the senses experience things), and other functions.

Long-term use of marijuana may cause emotional and physical changes. Yet perhaps its greatest danger is as a "gateway drug," meaning the user feels encouraged to try more serious and harmful drugs.

COCAINE

Cocaine is a stimulant of the nervous system, meaning it makes nerves especially active. For a short while, the user may feel very energetic, restless, and powerful. Yet soon after, the user feels uncomfortable and depressed—and craving the drug again.

With repeated use, cocaine can cause heart disease and mental illness. Cocaine has caused many deaths.

BARBITURATES

These drugs depress, or lessen the activity of, the nervous system. They once were popular treatments for anxiety and sleep disorders. But repeated use will lead to physical tolerance and addiction.

OPIATES

These drugs include morphine and heroin. Morphine is a pain-killing drug often prescribed to surgical patients. Heroin has no medical use and is illegal. All opiates are very addictive and can damage the nervous system with repeated use. They can also cause heart failure and death.

OTHER DRUGS

Even a medicine that a doctor prescribes can cause damage if it is used improperly. Pain killers, diet drugs, and doctor-approved steroids can each be abused, often when patients share their medications with others.

Even a single dose of cocaine, heroin, or other dangerous drugs can be fatal.

Emotional Health

The mind and body are connected, and each affects the other. **A healthy mind is just as important as a healthy body.** Just as good habits can help keep your body healthy, they can help you stay emotionally healthy, too.

Stress

Stress is a part of everyone's life. Examples include the feeling of pressure before a test or performance, changing schools, or losing a close friend or family member.

Yet sometimes stress can be severe and long-lasting. Stress that continues without relief can make it difficult to accomplish goals, and it can damage many body systems.

Activities that relieve stress focus the mind on something new or help it relax. Listening to music, reading a book, or writing in a journal are all good activities to try. So is any form of physical exercise.

DEPRESSION

Everyone feels sad sometimes. **Depression** is a feeling of sadness or hopelessness that does not leave on its own. Signs of depression include lack of interest in daily life, withdrawal from friends and family, and changes in eating or sleeping habits.

Depression can lead to suicide—one of the main causes of death among teens. Fortunately, depression can be treated and cured. A doctor, school counselor, or another trusted adult can help answer your questions about depression or any emotional health issue.

A good friend or trusted adult can act as a mediator to help resolve a conflict.

Conflict resolution

Teens may have conflicts with parents, teachers, classmates, and even good friends. Conflicts may be resolved in many ways, but violence is not one of them. Violence always causes more problems than it solves.

A better choice is to talk about a conflict. Sometimes a **mediator** can help. A mediator is someone who has no stake in the conflict, but helps both sides find an agreement.

Summary

- Proper care for the human body includes keeping clean, eating a healthful diet, daily exercise, and avoiding dangerous drugs and other substances.

- The human body progresses through the stages of infancy, childhood, adolescence, and adulthood. Each stage brings specific changes and challenges.

- Germs cause communicable diseases, meaning diseases that can be caught. Noncommunicable diseases (ones that cannot be caught) include arthritis, diabetes, cancer, and inherited diseases. Inherited diseases include cancer and alcoholism, among others.

- Good hygiene helps stop the spread of germs, while medicines and medical treatments can help the body fight diseases.

- A balanced diet provides the wide variety of nutrients that the body needs.

- Alcohol, tobacco, and many illegal drugs are addictive, meaning the body comes to depend on them. Teens are especially prone to these addictions.

Quiz

1 During which year of life does the body change the most?

   a. Age 0 to 1
   b. Age 5 to 6
   c. Age 12 to 13
   d. Age 24 to 25

2 What causes a communicable disease?

   a. germs
   b. inherited genes
   c. a poor diet
   d. worn-out body parts

3 Breads, cereals, and pasta are good sources of _____.

   a. protein
   b. fats and oils
   c. carbohydrates
   d. calcium and other minerals

4 A healthy exercise plan should include which types of exercise?

   a. aerobic only
   b. anaerobic only
   c. aerobic and anaerobic
   d. team sports only

5 Tobacco contains _____, an addictive drug that stimulates the nervous system.

   a. alcohol
   b. amphetamines
   c. nicotine
   d. tar

6 Which kind of drugs or medicines can be abused?

   a. opiates and barbiturates only
   b. illegal drugs only
   c. prescription medicines only
   d. any type of drug or medicine

Find the answers on page 47

Glossary

acne skin lesions, or pimples

addictive promoting the desire or need for further use of a substance or activity

adolescence stage of human development during which the body develops many characteristic male or female traits

aerobic exercise physical exercise that helps muscles use oxygen to release energy

alcoholism disease that involves physical and emotional dependence on alcohol

amino acid molecules that are critical to life and play a role in metabolism

anabolic steroids drugs that artificially build up muscles, but with dangerous side effects

anaerobic exercise intense exercise that helps build up muscle mass

antibiotic a medicine that slows the growth of, or destroys, microorganisms such as bacteria

antibody blood protein produced by the body in response to invading microorganisms or foreign substances in the body

bacteria large group of single-celled, microscopic organisms

calorie unit used to measure the energy in food

cell tiny, basic unit of life, present in all living things

chemical reaction natural reactions in the body, which happen in order to complete tasks

chemotherapy treatment used to kill cancer cells

cholesterol natural compound found in most body tissues. Some forms of cholesterol are thought to be harmful in larger amounts.

circulatory system body system responsible for circulating blood throughout the body. The system includes the heart, blood vessels, and the blood.

communicable disease disease caused by a germ or similar agent, and may be transferred from person to person.

depression long-lasting feeling of sadness or hopelessness

dietary fiber material in food that moves through the digestive tract and is not taken in by the body

drug any substance that changes how the body functions

embryo for humans, a growing mass of cells that will develop into a fetus

enamel the hard outer layer of a tooth

estrogen hormone that triggers the development of characteristic female traits

fetus stage of a developing baby from about 8 weeks until birth

gene unit of inheritance that controls or helps control a specific trait

gingivitis infection of the gums

hormone substance that travels through the blood and acts like a chemical messenger from one organ to another

hygiene set of practices that keep the body clean and promote health

immune system specialized white blood cells that recognize and attack germs. It is also called the third line of defense.

lactose the sugar in milk

mediator someone who is not involved in, or has no stake in, a conflict, and works to help both sides find a solution

medicine drug intended to improve body functions

menopause time in a woman's life when the menstrual cycle stops

menstrual cycle monthly cycle of the female reproductive system, also called a period

molecule tiny group of atoms

nervous system body system that includes the brain, spinal cord, and nerves

nicotine addictive drug in tobacco that stimulates the nervous system

noncommunicable disease disease that is not caused by germs and does not spread from person to person

nutrient material in food that the body needs and uses

nutritionist person who studies or is an expert in nutrition

organ functional unit of the body that is made from a variety of tissues. Examples include the heart, liver, and skin

organ system group of organs in the body that work together to accomplish a specific task, such as digesting food or circulating blood

organic compound chemical compound that contains carbon, and often is made or used by living things

organism individual living thing

over-the-counter describing medicines that adults can purchase without a doctor's order

physical fitness condition in which the body is strong, durable, and flexible

prescription medicine strong medicine that a doctor must order, or prescribe, for a patient

puberty time that adolescence begins

secondhand smoke smoke that enters the air from the use of a tobacco product

stimulate to excite, often referring to the body or the nervous system

testosterone hormone that triggers the development of characteristic male traits

tissue group of similar body cells that work together as a unit

trait physical or personality feature. Height and eye color are two physical human traits. Being shy or confident are personality traits.

tumor growth of body tissue that is not normal. Tumors are sometimes caused by cancer.

uterus chamber in the female reproductive system in which a developing baby grows and matures

vaccine treatment that prepares the immune system for reacting to a specific germ

Find Out More

Books

Ballard, Carol. *Food For Feeling Healthy*. Chicago: Heinemann Library, 2007.

Columbia University's Health Education Program. *The "Go Ask Alice" Book of Answers: A Guide to Good Physical, Sexual, and Emotional Health*. New York: Henry Holt and Company, 2006.

Hovius, Christopher. *The Best You Can Be: A Teen Guide to Fitness and Nutrition*. Bromall, P.A.: Mason Crest, 2005.

Kedge, Joanna; and Joanna Watson. *Fitness*. Chicago: Raintree, 2005.

Keegan, Kyle. *Chasing the High. A Firsthand Account of One Young Person's Experience with Substance Abuse*. New York: Oxford University Press, Inc., 2008.

McTavish, Sandra. *Life Skills: 225 Ready-to-Use Health Activities for Success and Well-Being*. San Fransisco: John Wiley and Sons, 2004.

Websites

KidsHealth.org
http://kidshealth.org/
This is an online encyclopedia devoted to health and the human body, with separate sections for kids, teens, and adults.

BAM! Body and Mind
http://www.bam.gov/
This huge website is crammed with ideas for staying healthy, eating right, and keeping physically fit.

It's My Life: Body
http://pbskids.org/itsmylife/body/index.html
From PBS comes this Web site devoted to the human body and good health.

Organizations

- The **American Heart Association** promotes cardiac health and fitness through programs, education, and research. Contact them at:

  American Heart Association
  National Center
  7272 Greenville Avenue
  Dallas, TX 75231

  Tel: (800) 242-8721

- **Al-anon**, and its affiliate for teens called **Alateen**, help people cope with a family member who abuses alcohol. They sponsor meetings in many communities.

  Al-Anon and Alateen
  1600 Corporate Landing Parkway
  Virginia Beach, VA 23454

  Tel: (757) 563-1600
  Email: wso@al-anon.org

- The mission of **Operation Respect** is to encourage children and teens to respect one another and be emotionally healthy. Contact them for free educational materials.

  Operation Respect
  2 Penn Plaza, 6th Floor
  New York, New York 10121

  Tel: (212) 904-5243
  Email: info@operationrespect.org

Quiz answers

1. a, **2.** a, **3.** c, **4.** c, **5.** c, **6.** d.

Index